D0880145

PENGUIN BOOKS

THE CAT INSIDE

William S. Burroughs was born on February 5, 1914 in St. Louis. A world-reknowned and influential writer, his numerous books include *Naked Lunch, Junky, Queer, Exterminator!, Nova Express, Interzone, The Wild Boys, The Ticket That Exploded, The Soft Machine, Port of Saints, The Burroughs File, The Adding Machine, The Third Mind* (with Brion Gysin), *The Cat Inside, The Letters of William S. Burroughs: 1945–1959, My Education, Ghost of Chance, Last Words*, and the trilogy *Cities of Red Night, The Place of Dead Roads*, and *The Western Lands*. In the course of his life Burroughs lived and wrote in New York City, Mexico City, Tangier, Paris, London, and Lawrence, Kansas, where he died on August 2, 1997. He loved cats.

William S. Burroughs

Penguin Books

The Cat

Inside

PENGUIN BOOKS

Published by the Penguin Group

Penguin Group (USA) Inc., 375 Hudson Street, New York, New York 10014, U.S.A.

Penguin Group (Canada), 10 Alcorn Avenue, Toronto,

Ontario, Canada M4V 3B2 (a division of Pearson Penguin Canada Inc.)

Penguin Books Ltd, 80 Strand, London WC2R 0RL, England

Penguin Ireland, 25 St Stephen's Green, Dublin 2, Ireland (a division of Penguin Books Ltd)

Penguin Group (Australia), 250 Camberwell Road, Camberwell,

Victoria 3124, Australia (a division of Pearson Australia Group Pty Ltd)

Penguin Books India Pvt Ltd, 11 Community Centre,

Panchsheel Park, New Delhi – 110 017, India

Penguin Group (NZ), cnr Airborne and Rosedale Roads,

Albany, Auckland, New Zealand (a division of Pearson New Zealand Ltd)

Penguin Books (South Africa) (Pty) Ltd, 24 Sturdee Avenue,

Rosebank, Johannesburg 2196, South Africa

Penguin Books Ltd, Registered Offices: 80 Strand, London WC2R 0RL, England

This edition first published in the United States of America by
Viking Penguin, a division of Penguin Books USA Inc. 1992
Published in Penguin Books 2002

16 18 20 19 17 15

The Cat Inside, in different form was published in a limited edition of 133
copies by The Grenfell Press in 1986, with eight illustrations by Brion Gysin,
including those that appear on the cover and title page of this edition.

THE LIBRARY OF CONGRESS HAS CATALOGED THE HARDCOVER EDITION AS FOLLOWS:
Burroughs, William S., 1914–
The cat inside / William S. Burroughs.
p. cm.
ISBN 0-670-84465-9 (hc.)
ISBN 0 14 20.0025 6 (pbk.)
1. Burroughs, William S., 1914– —Biography. 2. Novelists,
American—20th century—Biography. 3. Pet owners—United States—
Biography. 4. Cats—United States—Anecdotes. I. Title.
PS3552.U75Z464 1992
813'.54—dc20
[B] 92-1126

Printed in the United States of America
Set in Bembo   Designed by Kate Nichols

The Cat Inside

May 4, 1985. I am packing for a short trip to New York to discuss the cat book with Brion. In the front room where the kittens are kept, Calico Jane is nursing one black kitten. I pick up my Tourister. It seems heavy. I look inside and there are her other four kittens.

"Take care of my babies. Take them with you wherever you go."

I am selecting cat food at the pet shop in Dillon's supermarket and I meet an old woman. Seems her cats won't eat any cat food with fish in it. Well, I tell her, mine are just the opposite. They *prefer* the fishy foods like Salmon Dinner and Seafood Supper.

"Well," she says, "they certainly are company."

And what can she do for her company when there is no Dillon's and no pet shop? What can I do? I simply could not stand to see my little cats hungry.

Thinking back to early adolescence, I recall a recurrent sensation of cuddling some creature against my chest. It is quite small, about the size of a cat. It is not a human baby and it is not an animal. Not exactly. It is part human and part something else. I can recall an occasion in the house at Price Road. I must be twelve or thirteen. I wonder what it is . . . a squirrel? . . . not quite. I can't see it clearly. I don't know what it needs. I do know that it trusts me completely.

Much later I was to learn that I am cast in the role of the Guardian, to create and nurture a creature that is part cat, part human, and part something as yet unimaginable, which might result from a union that has not taken place for millions of years.

I have become in the last few years a dedicated cat lover, and now the creature is clearly recognized as a cat spirit, a Familiar. Certainly it partakes of the cat, and other animals as well: flying foxes, bush babies, the gliding lemurs with enormous yellow eyes that live in trees and are helpless on the ground, ringtailed lemurs and mouse lemurs, sables, raccoons, minks, otters, skunks and sand foxes.

Fifteen years ago I dreamt I had caught a white cat on a hook and line. For some reason I was about to reject the creature and throw it back, but it rubbed against me, mewling piteously.

Since I adopted Ruski, the cat dreams are vivid and frequent. Often I dream that Ruski has jumped onto my bed. Of course this sometimes happens, and Fletch is a constant visitor, jumping up on the bed and cuddling against me, purring so loud I can't sleep.

The Land of the Dead. . . . A reek of boiling sewage, coal gas and burning plastics . . . oil patches . . . roller coasters and Ferris wheels overgrown with rank weeds and vines. I can't find Ruski. I am calling his name . . . "Ruski! Ruski! Ruski!"

A deep feeling of sadness and foreboding.

"I shouldn't have brought him out here!"

I wake up with tears streaming down my face.

Last night I encountered a dream cat with a very long neck and a body like a human fetus, gray and translucent. I am cuddling it. I don't know what it needs or how to provide for it. Another dream years ago of a human child with eyes on stalks. It is very small, but can walk and talk. "Don't you want me?" Again, I don't know how to care for the child. But I am dedicated to protecting and nurturing him at any cost! It is the function of the Guardian to protect hybrids and mutants in the vulnerable stage of infancy.

Evidence indicates that cats were first tamed in Egypt. The Egyptians stored grain, which attracted rodents, which attracted cats. (No evidence that such a thing happened with the Mayans, though a number of wild cats are native to the area.) I don't think this is accurate. It is certainly not the whole story. Cats didn't start as mousers. Weasels and snakes and dogs are more efficient as rodent-control agents. I postulate that cats started as psychic companions, as Familiars, and have never deviated from this function.

Dogs started as sentinels. It is still their chief function in farm and village, to give notice of approach, as hunters and guards, and that is why they hate cats.

"Look at the services we provide and all cats do is loll around and purr. Ratters, are they? Take a cat half an hour to kill a mouse. All cats do is purr and alienate the Master's affections from my honest shit-eating face. Worst thing is they got no sense of right and wrong."

The cat does not offer services. The cat offers itself. Of course he wants care and shelter. You don't buy love for nothing. Like all pure creatures, cats are practical. To understand an ancient question, bring it into present time. My meeting with Ruski and my conversion to a cat man reenacts the relation between the first house cats and their human protectors.

Consider the variety of wild felines, many about the size of a house cat, some considerably larger and some much smaller, no larger as adults than a three-month-old house kitten. Of these cat strains many cannot be tamed at any age—so fierce and wild in their little cat spirits.

But patience, dedication and cross-breeding . . . two-pound hairless cats, sinuous as weasels, incredibly delicate, with long, thin legs, needle teeth, huge ears and eyes of a bright, amber color. This is but one of the exotic strains that fetch staggering prices in the cat markets . . . flying and gliding cats . . . a cat that is bright electric blue, giving off a faint smell of ozone . . . aquatic cats with webbed feet (he surfaces with a cutthroat trout in his jaws) . . . delicate, thin, light-boned swamp cats with large, flat paws—they can skim over quicksand and mud with incredible speed . . . tiny lemur cats with huge eyes . . . a scarlet, orange and green cat with reptile skin, a long, sinewy neck and poison fangs—the venom is related to that of the blue-ringed octopus: two steps and you fall on your face, an hour later you're dead . . . skunk cats with a deadly spray that kills in seconds like claws in the heart . . . and cats with poison claws squirting venom from a large gland in the center of the foot.

And there are my cats, engaged in a ritual that goes back thousands of years, tranquilly licking themselves after the meal. Practical animals, they prefer to have others provide the food . . . some of them do. There must have been a split between the cats who accepted domestication and those who did not. .

Back to present time with a weary sigh. There will be fewer and fewer exotic, beautiful animals. The Mexican hairless cat is already extinct. The tiny three-pound wild cats that can be easily tamed are always rarer, further away, plaintive lost spirits waiting for the human hand that will never come, fragile and sad as a boat of dead leaves launched in a park pond by a child. Or the phosphorescent bats that emerge once every seven years to fill the air with impossible riots of perfume . . . melodious, distant calls from the bat cats and gliding lemurs . . . the rain forests of Borneo and South America are going . . . to make way for what?

At Los Alamos Ranch School, where they later made the atom bomb and couldn't wait to drop it on the Yellow Peril, the boys are sitting on logs and rocks, eating some sort of food. There is a stream at the end of a slope. The counselor was a Southerner with a politician's look about him. He told us stories by the campfire, culled from the racist garbage of the insidious Sax Rohmer—East is evil, West is good.

Suddenly a badger erupts among the boys—don't know why he did it, just playful, friendly and inexperienced like the Aztec Indians who brought fruit down to the Spanish and got their hands cut off. So the counselor rushes for his saddlebag and gets out his 1911 Colt .45 auto and starts blasting at the badger, missing it with every shot at six feet. Finally he puts his gun three inches from the badger's side and shoots. This time the badger rolls down the slope into the stream. I can see the stricken animal, the sad shrinking face, rolling down the slope, bleeding, dying.

"You see an animal you kill it, don't you? It might have bitten one of the boys."

The badger just wanted to romp and play, and he gets shot with a .45 government issue. Contact *that*. Identify with *that*. Feel *that*. And ask yourself, whose life is worth more? The badger, or this evil piece of white shit?

As Brion Gysin says: "Man is a bad animal!"

A TV short on Bigfoot. Tracks and sightings in the Northwest mountain areas. Interviews with local inhabitants. Here is a three-hundred-pound female slob:

"What in your opinion should be done about these creatures if they exist?"

A dark shadow crosses her ugly face and her eyes shine with conviction. "Kill them! They might hurt somebody."

When I was four years old I saw a vision in Forest Park, St. Louis. My brother was ahead of me with an air rifle. I was lagging behind and I saw a little green reindeer about the size of a cat. Clear and precise in the late afternoon sunlight as if seen through a telescope.

Later, when I studied anthropology at Harvard, I learned that this was a totem animal vision and knew that I could never kill a deer. Later still, in the course of some film experiments with Antony Balch in London, I came to recognize the strange, still medium in which the green reindeer floats as a (comparatively) motionless subject projected in slow motion. Old photographer tricks.

Another vision at about the same age: I am awake at dawn in the attic room and see little gray men playing in my block house. They move very fast, like a 1920 speed-up film . . . whisk . . . they are gone. Just the empty block house in gray dawn light. I am motionless in this sequence, a silent witness.

The magical medium is being bulldozed away. No more green reindeer in Forest Park. The angels are leaving all the alcoves everywhere, the medium in which Unicorns, Bigfoot, Green Deer exist growing always thinner, like the rain forests and the creatures that live and breathe in them. As the forests fall to make way for motels and Hiltons and McDonald's, the whole magic universe is dying.

In 1982 I moved into a stone farmhouse five miles outside Lawrence. The house had been modernized with bath and propane heat and air conditioning. Modern and convenient. It was a long, cold winter. As spring came I glimpsed occasionally a gray cat shadow and put out food, which disappeared, but I could never get close to the gray cat.

Some time later I got my first clear glimpse of Ruski. Coming back from the barn with Bill Rich after a shooting session and he pointed: "There's a young cat." Glimpse of a lithe, purple-gray shape jumping down from the back porch. He was about six months old, a gray-blue cat with green eyes . . . Ruski.

It was an April evening, just before dark. I stepped out onto the back porch. At the far end of the porch was the first gray cat and beside him was a big white cat I had never seen before. Now the white cat starts towards me, rubbing himself against the table, slow, tentative. Finally he rolls at my feet, purring. Clearly the gray cat had brought him along to make the connection.

I thought the white cat was too forward and did not let him into the house. However, he returned two nights later and this time I did let him in.

May 3, 1982. This white cat would drive me insane if I had to live in the same apartment with it under my feet, rubbing against my leg, rolling on its back in front of me, leaping up on the table to paw at the typewriter. He's on top of the TV, he's on the chopping block, he's in the sink, he's pawing the telephone.

I am leaning against the sideboard having a drink. I think he is outside, then he jumps onto the sink and sticks his face an inch from mine. Finally I put him out and close the door . . . like an Arab boy who knows he is being naughty knows you will put him out sooner or later. No fuss, he just goes, fades down an alley in the gathering dusk and whisk, he is gone, leaving me feeling vaguely guilty.

I don't remember exactly when Ruski first came into the house. I remember sitting in a chair by the fireplace with the front door open and he saw me from fifty feet away and ran up, giving the special little squeaks I never heard from another cat, and jumped into my lap, nuzzling and purring and putting his little paws up to my face, telling me he wanted to be my cat.

But I didn't hear him.

There were three kittens born at the Stone House. The mother was a small black-and-white cat. Obviously the big white cat was the father. One kitten was an albino. The other two were predominantly white, except for their tails and paws, which were brown to black. The big gray male looked after the kittens as if they were his own. He was gray like Ruski, except for a white chest and stomach. I named him Horatio. He was a noble, manly cat, and had a strong, sweet nature.

Ruski hated the little cats. *He* was the cute little cat. They were interlopers. The one time I slapped Ruski was for attacking one of the kittens, and I have seen the mother drive him out of the barn when the kittens were there. And Ruski was terrified of Horatio. One evening on the back porch Horatio walked over to Ruski. (He wasn't Ruski then. I didn't yet know he was a Russian Blue. I called him Smoky.) He walked over in a casual but determined manner and lit into Smoke, who ran under the table.

I have observed that in cat fights the aggressor is almost always the winner. If a cat is getting the worst of a fight he doesn't hesitate to run, whereas a dog may fight to his stupid death. As my old jiujitsu instructor said, "If your trick no work, you better run."

May 8, 1982. Today the female cat killed a half-grown rabbit. I looked out through the picture window and saw her with this rabbit in her jaws which she dragged under the porch. James was horrified. Later, she was out on the porch licking the blood off her paws with a very satisfied expression. I don't care much for rabbits. They aren't cute at all, even the little ones. All they do is make stupid, galvanic attempts to get out of your hands, and big rabbits can give you a very nasty bite. I tried to retrieve the remains before they manifest themselves and start haunting the porch with the reek of carrion. I can see nothing from the accessible end of the porch and don't aim to crawl under there.

May 9, 1982. This morning I found what was left of the rabbit she killed . . . some fur and chewed bones strewn about the porch, gathering flies. The kittens did actually rip it apart and eat it. She takes her role as huntress, bringing meat for the young, very sincerely. The little cats romp about, pouncing on grasshoppers. They eat and sleep and play.

There is a kidney-shaped fish pool outside the picture window. I cleaned it out and put in some large goldfish I bought in a bait store. The cats are always trying to catch the fish, with no success. One time the white cat leapt for a frog across the pool. The frog dove in and the cat fell in. He is trouble-prone.

June 3, 1982. Perhaps I should do one of those sprightly "fixing up my country house" books . . . *First Year in the Garden* . . . a chapter on the White Cat who got his ass bit by a dog, and the gray cat . . . such a handsome animal. Smoky we call him, after Colonel Smoky, the narc in Maurice Helbrant's *Narcotic Agent,* bound with *Junkie* in the Ace edition . . . well, Smoky is getting to be a real nuisance, fawning all over me and putting his face up to mine, rubbing his head against my hand and following me around when I am trying to shoot. It's almost spooky. I am looking to find a good home for Smoky.

Reading over these notes, which were simply a journal of my year at the Stone House, I am absolutely appalled. So often, looking back over my past life, I exclaim: "My God, who is this?" Seen from here I appear as a most unsightly cartoon of someone who is awful enough to begin with . . . simpering, complacent, callous . . . "Got his ass bit by a dog." "Leaving one feeling vaguely guilty" . . . "like an Arab boy who knows he is being naughty" . . . snippy old English queen voice . . . "I am looking to find a good home for Smoky."

The white cat symbolizes the silvery moon prying into corners and cleansing the sky for the day to follow. The white cat is "the cleaner" or "the animal that cleans itself," described by the Sanskrit word *Margaras,* which means "the hunter who follows the track; the investigator; the skip tracer." The white cat is the hunter and the killer, his path lighted by the silvery moon. All dark, hidden places and beings are revealed in that inexorably gentle light. You can't shake your white cat because your white cat is you. You can't hide from your white cat because your white cat hides with you.

To me the white cat is a messenger who summons me to confront the horror of thermonuclear devastation as seen from the pet shop at Dillon's, chasing my cats through a wrecked house with a gun. The vision filled me with desolation and an iron resolve to prevent this big-power outrage. We need a miracle. Leave the details to Joe. . . .

Joe places a cat box on the board room table. Gently he removes a white cat. The board members crawl under the table, screaming, "THE WHITE CAT! THE WHITE CAT!"

A Nazi initiation into the upper reaches of the SS was to gouge out the eye of a pet cat after feeding the cat and cuddling it for a month. This exercise was designed to eliminate all traces of pity-poison and mold a full *Übermensch*. There is a very sound magical postulate involved: the practitioner achieves superhuman status by performing some atrocious, revolting, subhuman act. In Morocco, magic men gain power by eating their own excrement.

But dig out Ruski's eyes? Stack bribes to the radioactive sky. What does it profit a man? I could not occupy a body that could dig out Ruski's eyes. So *who* gained the whole world? I didn't. Any bargain involving exchange of qualitative values like animal love for quantitative advantage is not only dishonorable, as wrong as a man can get, it is also foolish. Because *you* get nothing. You have sold your *you*.

"Well, how does a beautiful young red-haired body grab you?" Yes, He will always find a sucker like Faust, to sell his soul for a strap-on. You want adolescent sex, you have to pay for it in adolescent fear, shame, confusion. In order to enjoy something you have to be there. You can't just sweep in for dessert, dearie.

I remember the one time I ever slapped Ruski for attacking one of the kittens. The way he looked at me, the shock and hurt, was identical with the look I got from my amigo Kiki. I was sleepy and petulant. He came in and started pushing at me, and finally I slapped him. In both cases I had to make amends. Ruski disappeared but I knew where he was. I went out to the barn and found him and brought him back. Kiki sat there with a tear in the corner of his eye. I apologized and finally he came around.

The big white cat became the first house cat and he and Ruski would sleep together on the same couch in brotherly acceptance. One day the big white cat came back with an ugly wound, evidently from a dog. The teeth had torn through his flesh on both sides of the tailbone as he was running and he managed to shake free or climb a tree. I blame myself now for not taking him to a vet. I merely rubbed on some penicillin ointment and he seemed to be on the road to recovery. Then one day he disappeared and was never seen again.

A car? A dog? A coyote? Perhaps another home?

"I think he's dead, Bill," James said.

There are crucial moments in any relationship, turning points. I had been away for ten days at Naropa. During my absence Bill Rich went out every day to feed the cats.

I have returned. Late afternoon on the back porch. I see Ruski and he moves away. Then he rolls on his side, tentative, not quite sure. I scoop him up and sit down on the edge of the porch. There is a clear moment when he recognizes me and begins squeaking and purring and nuzzling. In that moment I finally know that he is my cat, and decide to take him with me when I leave the Stone House.

One day at the Stone House, before any of the cats had come to live indoors, I was shooting out in the barn and I looked up and there atop the woodpile behind my target was the little white kitten. I holster my shooting iron and walk over slow, and now I can see the mother cat there on top of the woodpile with three little kittens around her. She sashays over to me and lays her head in my hand.

"I can see you're a good man, Sheriff. Take care of me and my babies."

It was very touching, the simplicity of the gesture. Thousands of years of female cats in that gesture, and the babies behind her: "This is my creation . . . all I can do . . . what I have to do."

For those of you who've not lived in the country (I mean real farm country, not the Hamptons), a word about barn cats. Most farms have barn cats to keep the mice and rats down. These cats are minimally fed on skimmed milk and table scraps. Otherwise they don't hunt. Of course it often happens that a barn cat becomes a house cat. And that is what every barn cat, every street cat wants. I find this desperate attempt to win a human protector deeply moving.

I wonder if dogs and cats leave signs like hoboes:

WATCH OUT FOR DOG.

STAY AWAY FROM THIS PLACE. OLD NUT WITH
    GUN.

GOOD FOR A HANDOUT.

And stars like a Michelin guide:

FOOD CLOTHES MONEY AND SMOKES. A PRINCE.

CHOW AND DRINK. A KING.

I noticed no stray dogs came around the Stone House:

FUCKING *CAT HOUSE*.

My lease at the Stone House was about to expire and I purchased a house in East Lawrence. Situated on an acre of wooded grounds on a quiet street, it is ideal for cats. A month before I moved, the white cat disappeared. Otherwise I would have taken him with me, since Ruski and the white cat coexisted in perfect harmony. I was sorry to leave Horatio behind, but he couldn't get along with Ruski and the female and the kittens needed him. The new tenant, Robert Sudlow, a well-known Kansas painter, promised to look after the cats who were staying.

Notes from early 1984: My connection with Ruski is a basic factor in my life. Whenever I travel, someone Ruski knows and trusts must come and live in the house to look after him and call the vet if anything goes wrong. I will cover any expense.

When Ruski was in the hospital with pneumonia I called every few hours. I remember once there was a long pause and the doctor came on to say, "I'm sorry, Mr. Burroughs" . . . the grief and desolation that closed around me. But he was only apologizing for the long wait. . . . "Ruski is doing fine . . . temperature down . . . I think he's going to make it." And my elation the following morning: "Down almost to normal. Another day and he can go home."

ED IS MISSING. LOVED ALBINO CAT WHITE ALL OVER. EYES ARE WHITE AND PINKISH. WEARING FLEA COLLAR. REWARD. CALL 841-3905.

I miss Ed more for his acts of mischief than his endearing moments. Yesterday I had bought cat food. (Ed has been missing now for about twenty-four hours. No, more like forty-eight now. We got back from Paris on Friday the thirteenth and he had just slipped away two hours before that.) I used to put the cans of cat food on the windowsill over the sink and Ed would get up on the sill and knock the cans down into the sink. A terrible clatter would wake me up. What have you done now, Ed? A broken dish, a glass knocked to the floor and broken . . . So I started to put the cans into the cabinet, where he wouldn't have access. Now, as I am taking the cat food out of my shopping bag, I look at the sill and think, Well, I can put the cans up there now. And at this moment I feel a sharp pang of loss, the loss of a loved presence, however small . . . the little cry he made when I carried him away from bothering Ruski . . . a pang of loss, of absence, the loss of my little white monkey beast (as I called him). He was always into everything. I'd open the drawer where the cutlery was kept and he would climb up and slide into the drawer. Where is he now? I have put the cat food cans back on the window, still hoping he will come back and knock them over. And the last two nights I've kept the porch lights on.

I remember the first sighting of Ed. James pointed under the back porch: "I see a little tiny white kitten." He tried to grab the cat to bring it into the house, but it yowled and splashed through the pond. Later, when I was feeding the three kittens, Ed was tractable and would purr in my lap as I stroked him. When we left the Stone House, James and Ira took Ed to live in their apartment on Louisiana Street. He grew up as a house cat, no contact with the outside. Then he was moved here to my house. There was trouble between him and Ruski, and talk of giving Ed to Phil Heying or someone else. I was very reluctant to see him go, hoping that he would adjust and get along with Ruski. Clearly he was starved for contact with another cat. He would lick Ruski's face.

The sight of Ed's empty food bowl . . . He was always fed from a small bowl in the front room. Ed's little white food bowl, with green trimming around the rim, bits of dried cat food stuck to the sides, is still on a shelf in the front room.

The ancient Egyptians went into mourning for the loss of a cat and shaved their eyebrows. And why shouldn't the loss of a cat be as poignant and heartfelt as any loss? Small deaths are the saddest, sad as the death of monkeys.

Toby Tyler cuddles the dying monkey in his arms.

The old farmer stands by the unfinished wall.

The pictures are engravings in old books.

The books crumble to dust.

August 9, 1984, Thursday. My relationship with my cats has saved me from a deadly, pervasive ignorance. When a barn cat finds a human patron who will elevate him to a house cat, he tends to overdo it in the only way he knows: by purring and nuzzling and rubbing and rolling on his back to call attention to himself. Now I find this extremely touching and ask how I could ever have found it a nuisance. All relationships are predicated on exchange, and every service has its price. When the cat is sure of his position, as Ruski is now, he becomes less demonstrative, which is as it should be.

I remember a white cat in Tangier at 4 calle Larachi, first cat to get in the house . . . he disappeared. And a beautiful white cat on a red mud wall at sunset, looking out over Marrakech. And a white cat in Algiers, across the river from New Orleans. I remember a faint, plaintive *meeoouw* at twilight. The cat was vmmery sick, lying under the kitchen table. He died during the night.

The next morning at breakfast (were the boiled eggs just right?) when I put my foot under the table the cat was stiff and cold. And I spelled it out for Joan, to avoid traumatizing the children: "The white cat is D–E–A–D." And Julie looked at the dead cat blankly and said, "Take him outside, because he stinks."

A cocktail joke for the *New Yorker* set. It isn't funny anymore . . . thin stray cat thrown out with the garbage. The white cat in Mexico City: I slapped it across the face with a book. I can see the cat running across the room to hide under a lumpy junked armchair. I can hear the cat's ears ringing from the blow. I was literally hurting myself and I didn't know it.

Then the dream in which a child showed me his bleeding finger and I indignantly demanded to know who had done this. The child beckoned me into a dark room and pointed the bleeding finger at me and I woke up crying "No! No! No!"

I don't think anyone could write a completely honest autobiography. I am sure no one could bear to read it: *My Past Was an Evil River.*

Animal contact can alter what Castaneda calls "assemblage points." Like mother-love. It's been slobbered over by Hollywood. Andy Hardy goes down on his knees by his mother's bed. What's wrong with that? A decent American kid praying for his mother. What's wrong with that?

"I'll tell you what's wrong with it, B.J. It's shit. It's dead mawkish muck and it destroys the truth under it."

Here is a mother hooded seal on an ice floe with her cub. Thirty-mile-an-hour winds, thirty degrees below zero. Look into her eyes, slitted, yellow, fierce, crazed, sad and hopeless. End line of a doomed planet. She can't lie to herself, she can't pull any pathetic rags of verbal self-glorification about her. There she is, on this ice floe with her cub. She shifts her five-hundred-pound bulk to make a dug available. There's a cub with its shoulder ripped open by one of the adult males. Probably won't make it. They all have to swim to Denmark, fifteen hundred miles away. Why? The seals don't know why. They have to get to Denmark. They all have to get to Denmark.

Someone said that cats are the furthest animal from the human model. It depends upon whát breed of humans you are referring to, and of course what cats. I find cats uncannily human on occasion.

In 1963 Ian Sommerville and I had just moved into the house at 4 calle Larachi in Tangier. Several cats assemble in the open door, slinking back and forth but afraid to come within reach. One white cat inches forward. I put out my hand. The cat arches his back, moving back and forth and purring under my hand as cats have done since the first cat was tamed.

. The other cats growl and whine in protest: "Front-office brown nose!"

August, 1984. James was downtown at Seventh and Massachusetts when he heard a cat mewling very loudly as if in pain. He went over to see what was wrong and the little black cat leapt into his arms. He brought it back to the house and when I started to open a tin of cat food the little beast jumped up onto the sideboard and rushed at the can. He ate himself out of shape, shit the litter box full, then shit on the rug. I have named him Fletch. He is all flash and glitter and charm, gluttony transmuted by innocence and beauty. Fletch, the little black foundling, is an exquisite, delicate animal with glistening black fur, a sleek black head like an otter's, slender and sinuous, with green eyes.

After two days in the house he jumped onto my bed and snuggled against me, purring and putting his paws up to my face. He is an unneutered male about six months old with splashes of white on his chest and stomach.

I kept Fletch in the house for five days lest he run away, and when we let him out he scuttled forty feet up a tree. The scene has a touch of Rousseau's *Carnival Evening* . . . a smoky moon, teenagers eating spun sugar, lights across the midway, a blast of circus music and Fletch is forty feet up and won't come down. Shall I call the fire department? Then Ruski goes up the tree and brings Fletch down.

A year later Ruski's son by Calico Jane is stuck up the same tree. It is getting dark. I can see him up there with my flashlight, but he won't come down, so I call Wayne Propst, who is coming with a ladder. I go out and shine my light up the tree and see Fletch's red collar. And Fletch brings the little cat down.

I award Fletch a four-star cuteness rating. Like most qualities, cuteness is delineated by what it isn't. Most people aren't cute at all, or if so they quickly outgrow their cuteness. . . . Elegance, grace, delicacy, beauty, and a lack of self-consciousness: a creature who knows he is cute soon isn't. . . . Diminutive size: a leopard is too big and too dangerous to be cute. . . . Innocence and trust. I remember forty years ago in my East Texas pot patch I looked up from examining a plant and there was a baby skunk. I reached out and stroked it and it looked at me with complete trust.

One of the cutest animals on earth is a sand fox. He can barely overpower a mouse. He shits with fear at the sight of a gopher. Mostly he lives on eggs, creeps into the hen house like a little gray ghost . . . SWAAAALKK! Too late. He has eaten an egg and skittered away. The bolder ones prey on young birds all hairless in the nest. Quick and furtive, he sneaks in with a worm in his teeth and they think it's Mother there with the worm and open their little yellow mouths. He bites through the throat and sucks the blood avidly, tearing off mouthfuls of breast, his eyes shine with joy, blood on his little black snout and his little white needle teeth like a greedy schoolboy tearing into a sweet. Almost disgusting. Redeemed by beauty and innocence he belches, spewing strawberry sauce across the headmaster's shirt.

"I say, I'm awfully sorry and all that rot. Won't happen again. Just let me clean you up, sir." He rushes out and comes back with a stale mop dripping dirty water and shoves the reeking mop at the headmaster. "Have you all neat and tidy in no time, guv." He slops garbage water all over the stunned headmaster. "Bloody loose ship they run here if you don't mind me saying so, sir. Why, Gor blimey, some of that muck got up into your dish, mate." He slaps the headmaster in the face, knocking him out of his chair.

An English cat hater of the upper classes confided to me that he had trained a dog to break a cat's back with one shake. And I remember he caught sight of a cat at a party and snarled out through the long yellow horse teeth that crowded out his mouth, "Nasty stinking little beast!" I was impressed by his class at the time and knew nothing of cats. Now I would get up from my chair and say, "Pawdon me, old thing, if I toddle along, but there's a nasty stinking big beast here."

I will take this occasion to denounce and excoriate the vile English practice of riding to hounds. So the sodden huntsmen can watch a beautiful, delicate fox torn to pieces by their stinking dogs. Heartened by this loutish spectacle, they repair to the manor house to get drunker than they already are, no better than their filthy, fawning, shit-eating, carrion-rolling, baby-killing beasts.

Warning to all young couples who are expecting a blessed event: *Get rid of that family dog.*

"What! Our Fluffy harm a child? Why that's ridiculous!"

Long may your child live to think so, little mother . . . fondly dandling their child and drooling baby talk when Fluffy, in a jealous rage, rushes on the baby, bites through its skull and kills it.

Dogs are the only animal other than Man with a knowledge of right and wrong. So Fluffy knows what to expect when he is dragged whimpering from under the bed where he cowers. He realizes the full extent of his trespass. No other animal would make the connection. Dogs are the only self-righteous animal.

Accidentally kicked Fletch, who was sleeping in the doorway to my room. He started to run. I carried him back and laid him on the bed and soon he was purring, then sleeping on his back. His face is something between a bat and a cat and a monkey . . . the top of his head a sleek, glistening black, the ears fuzzy and bat-like. The face with its black snout and long, expressive lips, like a sad monkey. Easy to imagine a Bat Cat, its leathery black wings glistening, sharp little teeth, glowing green eyes. His whole being radiates a pure, wild sweetness, flitting through night woods with little melodious cries, on some cryptic errand. There is also an aura of doom and sadness about this trusting little creature. He has been abandoned many times over the centuries, left to die in cold city alleys, in hot noon vacant lots, pottery shards, nettles, crumbled mud walls. Many times he has cried for help in vain.

Purring in his sleep, Fletch stretches out his little black paws to touch my hands, the claws withdrawn, just a gentle touch to assure him that I am there beside him as he sleeps. He must have a dream image of me. Cats are said to be color-blind: grainy black-and-white, a flickering silver film full of rents as I leave the room, come back, go out, pick him up, put him down. Who could harm such a creature? Train his dog to kill him! Cat hate reflects an ugly, stupid, loutish, bigoted spirit. There can be no compromise with this Ugly Spirit.

I have eulogized the fennec fox, a creature so delicate and timorous in the wild state that he dies of fright if touched by human hands. The red fox, the silver fox, the bat-eared fox of Africa . . . all beautiful beasts. Wolves and coyotes in the wild condition are acceptable. What went so hideously wrong with the domestic dog? Man molded the domestic dog in his own worst image . . . self-righteous as a lynch mob, servile and vicious, replete with the vilest coprophagic perversions . . . and what other animal tries to fuck your leg? Canine claims to our affection reek of contrived and fraudulent sentimentality. The Old Shepherd's chief mourner. Took three days to find the old fart and by then the dog had eated his face off. Looks up with a shit-eating grin and rolls in carrion.

I am not a dog hater. I do hate what man has made of his best friend. The snarl of a panther is certainly more dangerous than the snarl of a dog, but it isn't ugly. A cat's rage is beautiful, burning with a pure cat flame, all its hair standing up and crackling blue sparks, eyes blazing and sputtering. But a dog's snarl is *ugly*, a redneck lynch-mob Paki-basher snarl . . . snarl of someone got a "Kill a Queer for Christ" sticker on his heap, a self-righteous occupied snarl. When you see that snarl you are looking at something that has no face of its own. A dog's rage is not his. It is dictated by his trainer. And lynch-mob rage is dictated by conditioning.

Thursday, October 4, 1984. Ugly, senseless, hysterical hatred is extremely frightening in animals or people. My dreams were haunted by archetypical dog packs. . . . I am in an oval cul-de-sac at the end of a long, soft tunnel. At the far end of this chamber there is a strong magnetic pull. Get too close and it will pull you into the womb. I step back just in time. Allen Ginsberg is at my side with a mantra: "Closing that old Womb Door, don't wanna go back no more." Then I hear a baying sound, muffled by the soft walls of the passage, but unmistakable: "THE DOGS! THE DOGS!" Closer now, a snarling, slavering Cerberus pack. So Allen pulls an Indian rope trick to erect a scaffold, but it isn't quite high enough and I wake up kicking at the dogs as they leap up to drag me down.

The time to pet a cat is when the cat is eating. That is not the time to pet a dog. It is good to pet a sleeping cat. He stretches and purrs in sleep. Better let sleeping dogs lie. I remember at the poetry festival in Rome, John Giorno and I are going down to breakfast. A big dog is sleeping on a landing.

"This is a very friendly dog," John said, and bent down to pet the beast, who growled ominously and showed his yellow teeth.

September 12, 1984. Sometimes Fletch will bite me petulantly when I try to carry him away from a play scene he wants to continue. Not hard enough to hurt, just an irritable teenage nip . . . "Leave me alone! I want to play!" A few minutes ago he knew I was going to put him out and he didn't want to go so he crawled under a low desk where I couldn't reach him. Such human child reactions.

I have said that cats serve as Familiars, psychic companions. "They certainly are company." The Familiars of an old writer are his memories, scenes and characters from his past, real or imaginary. A psychoanalyst would say I am simply projecting these fantasies onto my cats. Yes, quite simply and quite literally cats serve as sensitive screens for quite precise attitudes when cast in appropriate roles. The roles can shift and one cat may take various parts: my mother; my wife, Joan; Jane Bowles; my son, Billy; my father; Kiki and other amigos; Denton Welch, who has influenced me more than any other writer, though we never met. Cats may be my last living link to a dying species.

And Calico Jane is well cast as Jane Bowles . . . so delicate, refined and special. (In a beach restaurant in Tangier an ugly, dirty little urchin nudged her and held out his grubby little hand. "Oh, no!" she said. "I only like old men.") The little cat has real class, and so like her to be a calico somehow.

I was present when Jane was born. She was the first to lap milk and the first to eat solid food. She was the last to purr. (Wimpy was the first.) She seemed almost catatonic, and developed slowly. Now she purrs and snuggles against me in a delicate way . . . a ladylike way. Janie does things in a ladylike way.

Joan didn't like to have her picture taken. She almost always kept out of group photos. Like Mother, she had an elusive, ethereal quality.

For the last four years of her life, Mother was in a nursing home called Chateins in St. Louis. "Sometimes she recognizes me. Sometimes she doesn't," my brother, Mort, reported. During those four years I never went to see her. I sent postcards from time to time. And six months before she died I sent a Mother's Day card. There was a horrible, mushy poem in it. I remember feeling "vaguely guilty."

This cat book is an allegory, in which the writer's past life is presented to him in a cat charade. Not that the cats are puppets. Far from it. They are living, breathing creatures, and when any other being is contacted, it is sad: because you see the limitations, the pain and fear and the final death. That is what contact means. That is what I see when I touch a cat and find that tears are flowing down my face.

Fletch, the brat cat, the boy cat who paws down tapestries. He just now jumped up on the table where I was reading. Then, irritated by cigarette smoke from the ashtray, he jumped against a chair where I had draped my coat, and knocked the chair over. It was quite deliberate. The lovable little demon cat. And so sad in his limitations, his dependence, his pathetic little histrionic gestures.

The thought of anyone mistreating him! He has been mistreated so many times over the centuries, my little black Fletch with his glistening coat and his amber eyes. The way he will suddenly rush into the room while I am lying down in laziness and disinclination to get on with the endless salt mines of *The Western Lands*. Jump on my chest and snuggle against me and put his paws up to my face. Other times his eyes are all black pupil, as sure an indication of "Watch out!" as a horse with its ears laid back. Then he will bite and scratch.

Ginger plays Pantapon Rose, an old madame in a St. Louis sporting house on Westminster. She always shunted me into a curtained alcove on the way out, lest I meet one of my father's friends on the way in. A hard, practical woman from a farm family in the Ozarks. Ginger was Ruski's old lady, always around. So I started feeding her and hoping she would go away. How American of me: "Who's that at the door? Give her some money. Send her away." Of course she didn't go away. Instead, she dropped four brown-orange kittens on the back porch, all replicas of herself. I doubt if Ruski was involved. My friend Patricia Marvin managed to give them all away without any fuss—one of the advantages of living in a small town. You get to know friendly, helpful people.

For a long while I wouldn't let Ginger in the house, but we had a cold wave down to fifteen below and when the temperature got below twenty I had to let her in, haunted by the thought of finding her frozen corpse on the porch. Ruski wouldn't stick his nose out the door. Her second pregnancy was during the following winter and she bore the kittens in the house, in a basket I had prepared for her. And of course she stayed in to nurse the kittens. When the kittens were ten weeks old I gave two of them away. And Ginger kept looking for them and crying from room to room, looking under the bed, under the couch. And I decided I couldn't go through this again. Ginger has been going through that for centuries.

I used to play with Ed, the albino cat,
get my little Ed!" and he rushes under
the sofa, under the bed, into the front room. It's a game that
children like, and they giggle and run. "Don't get me!"
Calico Jane likes to play this game. I used to play it with Billy
in the Algiers house: "Where's my Willy?"

In a dream I am in the house at 4664 Pershing Avenue
where I was born. On the second floor, at the entrance to my
old bedroom, I encounter a little blond child waiting there.
"Are you Billy?" I ask.

"I'm anybody to anybody who loves me," he answers.

There is Wimpy, the orange-white cat, on a chair by the bed. If I shut the door to my room he whines and paws at the door. He isn't hungry. He just wants to be near me or near somebody who loves him. Billy used to do that in the house on Wagner Street in Algiers. He would cry outside my door until I opened it. And the house was a lot like this house, a plain white-frame house, long and narrow.

I catch clear glimpses of Kiki through Ruski. I have felt Kiki right there when I pick up Ruski and he doesn't want to be picked up . . . "*¡Déjeme,* William! *Tú estás loco.*" And the time I slapped him . . . the averted face, downcast eyes . . . then he was gone. And of course I knew just where he was and carried him back to the house . . . "Thin stray cat used to be me, meester."

Kiki left me and went to Madrid. He had good reason to leave. Terminal junk at the time. He was stabbed to death in a hotel room by a jealous lover who found him with a girl.

Kiki in Tangier, Angelo in Mexico City . . . and someone else I cannot identify because he is so close to me. Sometimes he is there in my face and body, real as anybody could be, and he says, "IT'S ME, BILL . . . IT'S ME," over and over. That's the way it is with Ruski when he squeaks and puts his paws up to my face. He is not as demonstrative as he used to be. Sometimes he moves away from my hand . . . "You shame me, William. I am not a *niño.*" It can get quite creepy.

My first Russian Blue cat came from the streets of Tangier and found his way into the garden of the Villa Muniria, where I was staying in 1957. He was a beautiful tomcat with a lustrous gray-blue coat, like very expensive fur, and green eyes. Although he was a full-grown cat at the time he quickly became very affectionate and often spent the night in my room, which opened onto the garden. That cat would catch a piece of meat in the air between his front paws like a monkey. He looked exactly like Ruski.

Wimpy shows me flashes of my son, Billy, and my poor father. Ten o'clock in the house at Price Road. I go down to the pantry for milk and cookies, hoping my father won't be there. Frustration makes me surly and petulant. "Gay" was not a household word in those days.

He is there. "Hello, Bill."

The pathetic appeal and the hurt in his eyes.

"Hello."

Nothing but cold hate. If only . . . Too late. Over from Cobble Stone Gardens.

Another flashback: about two months before I left the Stone House. Sitting in the chair by the fireplace with the white cat in my lap, I feel a sudden twinge of hate and resentment. I am not at all sure of moving into a house. There isn't money! A small apartment most likely. Litter boxes . . . intolerable! I can smell them from here. Did the white cat disappear in that flash of resentment? People and animals may go away in spirit before they go away in body. If only the white cat were here now to jump up onto the desk and paw the typewriter.

Note from early April, 1985: Ruski crouches down with a beaten look. He whines sadly through the room, skitters away from me and down into the basement with his little cries. The cry of a half-formed mutant creature . . . hope withering . . . the cry of that hope dying. Ruski is now crying in the basement. Whenever I get close to him he cries and moves away. The mutant that doesn't quite make it, the only one of his kind, the little lost voice always fainter.

Down in the basement looking for Ruski. Nothing and nobody there but the stink of death, the dank old stagnant air, the gun cabinet, targets covered with dust.

Nuclear winter . . . howling wind and snow. An old man in a shack improvised from the ruins of his house huddles under torn comforters, blankets full of holes, and dirty rugs with his cats.

April 2, 1985. Ruski is on the desk by the north window. I pet him. He squeaks and nuzzles me and goes to sleep. I feel his sad, lost voice in my throat, stirring, aching. When you feel grief like that, tears streaming down your face, it is always a portent, a warning—danger ahead.

May 1, 1985. A feeling of deep sadness is always a warning to be heeded. It may refer to events which will happen in weeks, months, even years. In this case exactly one month.

Yesterday I walked up to the house on Nineteenth Street, depression and pain dragging every step. Ruski has not been to the house this morning.

Wednesday morning, May 1. I received Ruski's desperate call for help, the sad, frightened voice I first heard a month ago.

MAYDAY MAYDAY MAYDAY.

And I know where he is. I call the Humane Society.

"No. We have no cat of that description."

"Are you sure?"

"Wait, let me check again. . . ." (Cries of frightened animals.)

"Well, yes, we do have a cat of that description."

"I'll be right there."

"Well, you have to go to the city clerk with your certificate for rabies vaccination and pay a ten-dollar pickup fee."

All this accomplished in half an hour with the aid of David Ohle. We arrive at the animal shelter. The place is a death camp, haunted by the plaintive, despairing cries of lost cats waiting to be put to sleep.

"That is one scared cat!" the girl says as she leads me to "Holding," as it is called. Frozen with fear, Ruski cowers with another terrified cat on a steel shelf. She unlocks the door. I reach in and gently lift my cat into his box.

We have to wait fifteen minutes for the arresting officer before the cat can be released. He is out front when I come back with Ruski in the box. He is a young, blond police punk, skinny, with a scraggly mustache. Not even a policeman, quite. I ask him the circumstances of Ruski's arrest. He doesn't know. His partner made the collar. His partner's off today. The police shutter falls across his scrawny face.

"It's illegal to allow your cat to run free. Dogs and cats must be on the owner's premises and under verbal command at all times. It's the law." (A law habitually violated by everyone in Lawrence who has a yard.)

After seventy-two hours in Holding, the animals are put up for adoption. The animals know. Animals always know death when they see it. Better put your best paw forward. It's your last chance, Kitty.

What chance would Ruski have, a full-grown, un-neutered cat paralyzed with fear? One scared cat.

"Oh, Daddy, I want that one!" Little boy points to Ruski.

"Well, we wouldn't advise . . . he's not very responsive."

"Guess we'll pass on that one, Punky."

Ruski gives a meow of despair as they walk on.

I question the underlying assumption that one does a cat a favor by killing him . . . oh, sorry . . . I mean "putting him to sleep." Turn to backward countries that don't have Humane Societies for a simple alternative. In Tangier stray cats fend for themselves. I remember an eccentric old English lady in Tangier. Every morning she went to the fish market and filled a bag with cheap fish and made the rounds of vacant lots and other locales where stray cats congregated. I have seen as many as thirty cats rush up at her approach.

Well, why not? The money now spent on caging and killing cats could maintain actual shelters with food dispensers. Of course the cats would have to be neutered and vaccinated for rabies.

That night, for the first time in three years, Ruski jumped onto my bed purring and chittering, nuzzled against me and went to sleep thanking me for saving him.

Next day I called Animal Control. "My cat was picked up and taken to the shelter and I want to know the circumstances."

"The circumstances are that it's illegal to let your cat run free."

"No, I mean how did my cat happen to be picked up?"

It seems he was caught in an animal trap at Nineteenth and Barker, about two hundred yards from the back line of my property. Probably he had been shut in the box trap all night. No wonder he was a scared cat.

At the time I didn't know about animal traps. I didn't know that cats could be picked up. Close. Very close. Suppose I had been away. Suppose . . . I don't want to. It hurts. Now all my cats wear rabies tags.

The cry I heard through Ruski was not only his signal of distress. It was a sad, plaintive voice of lost spirits, the grief that comes from knowing you are the last of your kind. There can be no witness to this grief. No witnesses remain. It must have happened many times in the past. It is happening now. Endangered species. Not just those that actually exist, or existed at one time and died, but all the creatures that might have existed.

A hope. A chance. The chance lost. The hope dying. A cry following the only one who could hear it when he is already too far away to hear, an aching, wrenching sadness. This is a grief without witness. "You are the last. Last human crying." The cry is very old. Very few can hear it. Very painful. The chance was there for an enchanted moment. The chance was lost. Wrong turn. Wrong time. Too soon. Too late. To invoke all-out magic is to risk the terrible price of failure. To know that chance was lost because you failed. This grief can kill.

Life, such as it is, goes on. Dillon's is still open from seven a.m. to twelve midnight, seven days a week.

I am the cat who walks alone. And to me all super-markets are alike.

I am drinking Dillon's fresh-squeezed orange juice and eating farm-fresh eggs out of an egg cup I bought in Amsterdam. Wimpy rolls, nuzzling my feet, purring *I love you I love you I love you.* He loves me.

Meeeowww. "Hello, Bill."

The distance from there to here is the measure of what I have learned from cats.

There's the old cat lady feeding the cats on the French consulate grounds right opposite the Café de France. The cats rush forward, snapping fish in the air. My first Russian Blue caught meat in his paws. Don't remember what happened to him.

All you cat lovers, remember all the millions of cats mewling through the world's rooms lay all their hopes and trust in you, as the little mother cat at the Stone House laid her head in my hand, as Calico Jane put her babies in my suitcase, as Fletch jumped into James's arms and Ruski rushed towards me chittering with joy.

The Tangier smoke cat catches a piece of meat in his front paws like a monkey . . . my little white monkey beast. The white cat rubs his way towards me, tentative, hoping.

We are the cats inside. We are the cats who cannot walk alone, and for us there is only one place.

The Letters of William S. Burroughs, 1945–1959
This volume of correspondence vividly documents the personal and cultural history through which Burroughs developed, revealing clues to illuminate his life and keys to open up his text. Tracking his turbulent journey across two decades and three continents, these letters also give insight into the Beat generation as a whole.

ISBN 0-14-009452-0

My Education: A Book of Dreams
Hundreds of Burroughs's dreams—intense, vivid, visionary—form the spiraling core of this unique and haunting journey in to perception, which remains one of his most profoundly personal books.

ISBN 0-14-009454-7

Western Lands
Burroughs's eagerly awaited final novel in the trilogy begun with *Cities of the Red Night* and *The Place of Dead Roads* is a profound, revealing, and often astonishing meditation on mortality, loneliness, nuclear peril, and the inextinguishable hope for life after death.

ISBN 0-14-009456-3

FOR THE BEST IN PAPERBACKS, LOOK FOR THE

In every corner of the world, on every subject under the sun, Penguin represents quality and variety—the very best in publishing today.

For complete information about books available from Penguin—including Penguin Classics, Penguin Compass, and Puffins—and how to order them, write to us at the appropriate address below. Please note that for copyright reasons the selection of books varies from country to country.

In the United States: Please write to *Penguin Group (USA), P.O. Box 12289 Dept. B, Newark, New Jersey 07101-5289* or call 1-800-788-6262.

In the United Kingdom: Please write to *Dept. EP, Penguin Books Ltd, Bath Road, Harmondsworth, West Drayton, Middlesex UB7 0DA.*

In Canada: Please write to *Penguin Books Canada Ltd, 10 Alcorn Avenue, Suite 300, Toronto, Ontario M4V 3B2.*

In Australia: Please write to *Penguin Books Australia Ltd, P.O. Box 257, Ringwood, Victoria 3134.*

In New Zealand: Please write to *Penguin Books (NZ) Ltd, Private Bag 102902, North Shore Mail Centre, Auckland 10.*

In India: Please write to *Penguin Books India Pvt Ltd, 11 Panchsheel Shopping Centre, Panchsheel Park, New Delhi 110 017.*

In the Netherlands: Please write to *Penguin Books Netherlands bv, Postbus 3507, NL-1001 AH Amsterdam.*

In Germany: Please write to *Penguin Books Deutschland GmbH, Metzlerstrasse 26, 60594 Frankfurt am Main.*

In Spain: Please write to *Penguin Books S. A., Bravo Murillo 19, 1° B, 28015 Madrid.*

In Italy: Please write to *Penguin Italia s.r.l., Via Benedetto Croce 2, 20094 Corsico, Milano.*

In France: Please write to *Penguin France, Le Carré Wilson, 62 rue Benjamin Baillaud, 31500 Toulouse.*

In Japan: Please write to *Penguin Books Japan Ltd, Kaneko Building, 2-3-25 Koraku, Bunkyo-Ku, Tokyo 112.*

In South Africa: Please write to *Penguin Books South Africa (Pty) Ltd, Private Bag X14, Parkview, 2122 Johannesburg.*